Judy
FOR GIRLS 1991

Printed and Published in Great Britain by D. C. THOMSON & CO., LTD., 185 Fleet Street, London EC4A 2HS © D. C. THOMSON & CO., LTD., 1990. ISBN 0-85116-471-4

£3.40

See You Soon!

JILL EVANS went to Mountford Girls' School. One day, as she walked home—

There's Steve Bradshaw. He goes to the local boys' school. It looks like he's waiting for me. I wonder what he wants?

Jill soon found out!

Go out with you? Yes, I'd love to! Thanks, Steve.

Great!

My first ever date! I can hardly wait.

They arranged to go to the cinema—

CINEMA

We're a bit early. The film doesn't begin for another half-hour. But we can sit inside and chat.

That's fine by me!

So—: ...and I always listen to the local radio's morning pop programme. They play all the chart hits.

I like it too. The DJ's funny.

Yes! He really brightens me up in the mornings.

This is great! Steve and I seem to like all the same things. We're getting on really well.

The lights are going down now. The film's about to start.

I wonder if Steve will put his arm around me. I hope so!

But— He isn't taking any notice of me at all! He hasn't taken his eyes off the screen since the film started.

But— I enjoyed tonight! Maybe we could go out again some time? I'll be in touch! I've got your phone number.

Oh! Okay then. Thanks.

He must have liked me more than I thought. I hope he rings soon.

I feel really fed up. I'll bet he doesn't ask to see me again.

6

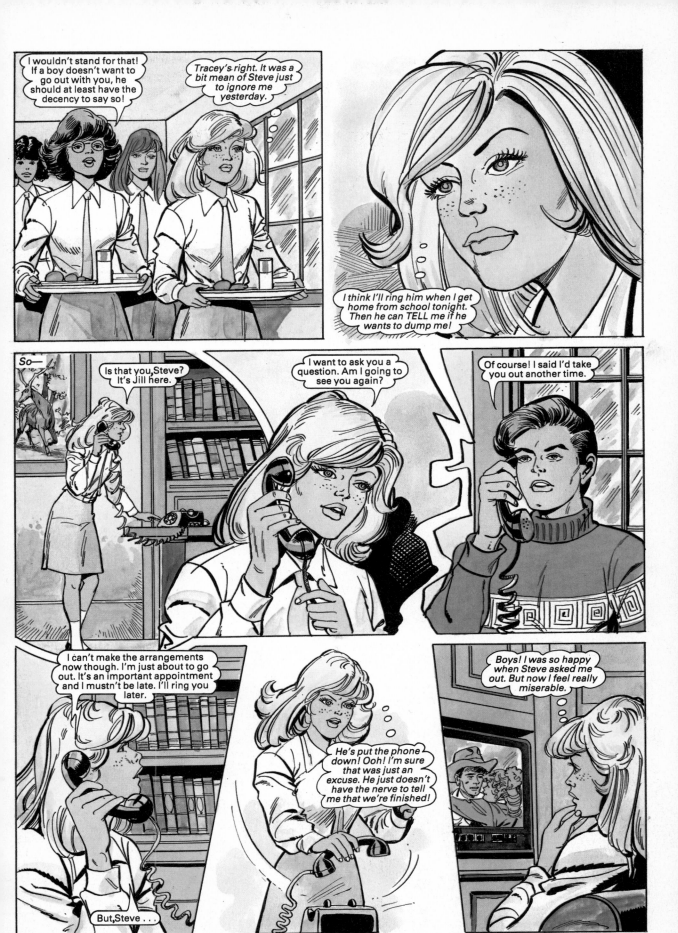

7

But, half an hour later—

Visitor for you, Jill.

STEVE!

Hi! I'm sorry I had to dash when you phoned earlier. But I had to get to the optician's before they closed.

The optician's? But you don't wear glasses.

I do now. I've just collected them. I've been waiting for them for a couple of weeks. I've had awful difficulty seeing things.

What? So that's why you ignored me yesterday when I waved at you!

Did I? I'm really sorry, Jill. I obviously didn't see you. No wonder you sounded so cross on the phone!

I understand why he had to concentrate so hard on the film now. He must have had difficulty seeing that too.

What a mess! But I'm glad it's all cleared up now. So, let's make arrangements for our next date!

Fine! I can SEE we're going to make the perfect couple!

THE End

10

On Monday, at lunch break—

Do me a favour, Janet. Go and see if I left my cardigan in the music room.

Very well, Miss Wright.

That's Trudy! I didn't know she could play the guitar as well as that.

Bravo! You're full of surprises, Trudy!

Oh, Janet! You startled me!

Trudy! Your guitar playing is brilliant!

It's only that I spend so much time at home practising.

Miss Wright, did you know Trudy could play the guitar?

Yes I did, and Mrs Larkin, the music head, would like us to persuade her to perform in our concert next week.

You MUST play at the concert, Trudy.

I . . . I'm not sure that I could play in front of a lot of people. I'll have to see what my mum says.

12

Continued on Page 39

13

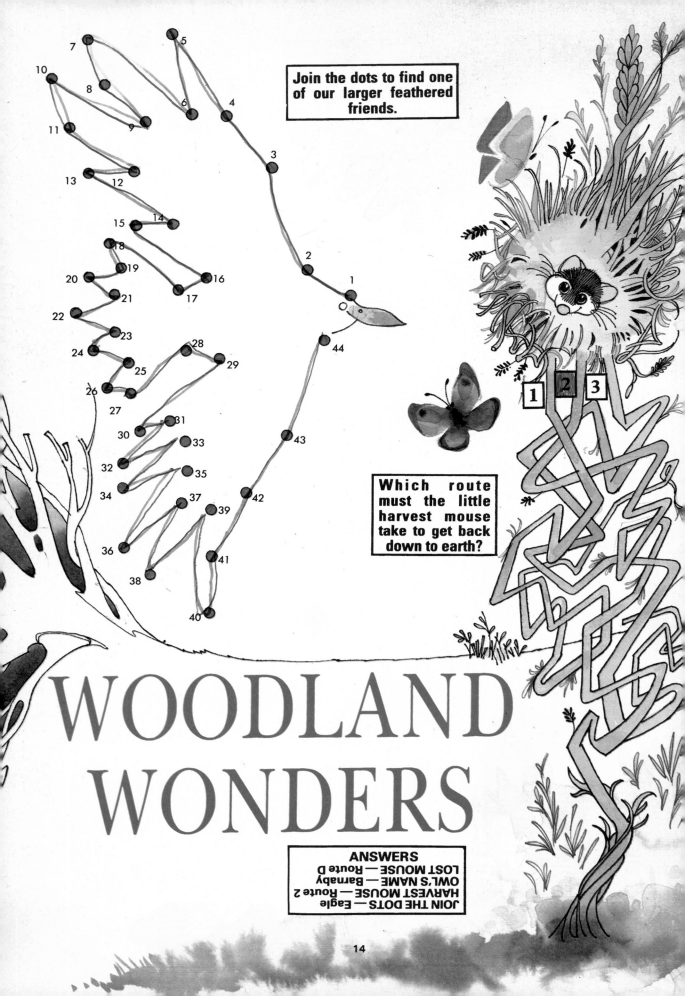

Join the dots to find one of our larger feathered friends.

Which route must the little harvest mouse take to get back down to earth?

WOODLAND WONDERS

Find the owl's name from these jumbled letters:

BARNABY

ANBRBYA

Which of the four routes must the mouse take to join his friends? He must not cross a black line.

Judy & Co.

Snow White. I'd love to see that.

A bit babyish isn't it?

Well, I'D feel a right fool!

Ready? Why don't we ask Judy if she wants to come?

Not really, Judy. It's a film for any age group.

Well, how about the two of US going to see it, Tracy?

You're on! We'll go tonight.

Okay. I'm sure she does really.

Sorry, girls, but Judy's not in. She volunteered to babysit for her little cousin.

Hey, isn't that Judy up ahead in the queue?

It looks like her. Let's go and see.

Judy VOLUNTEERED to babysit? She must be ill!

Thought you weren't coming to see this film?

Er...I...well, my little cousin here wanted to see it, so I had to bring him.

There! Now don't you dare tell anyone it was MY idea to come here!

16

Annie's Eyes

ELLIE CARTER was well known around Sallowfield Market. She earned her daily bread by running errands for the stallholders, who all had a soft spot for her.

Fetch me a hot pie, Ellie — and get one for yourself.

Ta, Charlie. You're a gent!

They all knew she could be trusted —

Come and watch the stall for ten minutes, Ellie. I know you won't pinch 'nuthin'.

I play fair with him 'cos I know he'll give me the left-over fruit and veg at the end of the day.

It's been a good day. I got a stale loaf, as well as the fruit and veg.

Well, well, if it ain't Ellie Carter! Remember the rules of our gang! Share and share alike.

You mean you want to pinch everything I earned today, Watt Dixon.

Catch 'er . . . OUCH!

One thing I've learned. You've got to be quick on your feet around here.

I think I've given 'em the slip, but I'll hide here for a while, just in case.

What in . . . ? Someone's dumped some kittens in that sack, I'll bet. It's moving and making funny sounds.

Poor little things! I reckon they deserve the chance to live, as much as anyone else.

H-HELP ME . . . !

You poor little nipper! Who did this to you?

Don't squeeze all the breath out of me, girl. What's your name?

My name's Annie! Please don't leave me!

Whoever you are, you're used to something better than this! That dress was posh once — and you've got real shoes!

You'd better come home with me for now, Annie what's-yer-name!

That's half-a-dozen times you've tripped up, girl. I suppose your legs are weak, from having been trussed up in that sack.

Here we are! It's no palace, but what do you think of it?

I . . . I don't know. I can't see!

What do you mean, you can't see? Cor — you're blind, aren't you?

My head hurts — I can't see. I don't know who I am . . .

There, there! Don't get into a state, Annie. First thing to do is have something to eat.

You must belong to SOMEONE. Until we find your real home, I'll be your eyes, Annie. I'll look after you.

Next morning —

While I'm working, I'll keep listening out for news of a lost little girl who might be you. Meanwhile, you try and remember how you got in that sack!

Y . . . yes, Ellie.

19

What are you doing now, Ellie?

I'm holding old Sam's horse while he goes for his dinner. He'll probably give us a bit of his bread and cheese, as wages.

What prize has Ellie Carter got for herself today? A skinny brat to look after.

Who's that, Ellie? I'm scared!

Just someone who's too big for his boots. Wait there, Annie. I'll see 'em off.

Hop it, Watt Dixon!

Ellie . . . help!

Someone grabbed me. They stole my shoes.

Oh, no! Sorry, Annie, those shoes will be sold before we can track 'em down.

Several days passed —

I've had an idea, Annie. Maybe you come from some of these posh houses. We'll walk round the places where the rich folk live, and I'll describe 'em to you. See if you recognise anything.

Several hours later —

I can't walk any further, Ellie. I still can't remember where I live. I think you'll have to be my eyes for ever and ever.

Let's go home. You're worn out.

Clever girl, Annie! This is our first clue to finding out who you really are. All we got to do is trace that toff in the black carriage.

But another two days passed —

It sounds like there are so many carriages. Can't you see the one we want?

It could take weeks, Annie. What we need are some more eyes to help. I'm going to put out the word that I need to speak to Watt Dixon.

You want me to join your gang, because I get more pickings from the market than any of you. Well, I agree — but you've got to help Annie first.

Ellie described the black carriage with the silver lamps —

I got members of my gang all over London. I'll pass the message round, and we'll find that carriage before morning.

Sure enough, next day —

You did well, Watt. I can manage from now.

Wait a minute, Ellie Carter. If there's a reward for returning this lost kid, then it's fair shares, remember?

Annabel — but you're DEAD!

Uncle Roderick!

Your memory's come back!

I remember everything! He became my guardian when my parents were drowned at sea. But one day I heard him boasting . . .

I arranged for my dear brother and his wife to perish by bribing the captain of the vessel. Now I am the child's guardian, it will be easy to get the estate signed over to me!

You murdered Mama and Papa! You're an evil, wicked man! *AAAH!*

Grab the brat! She'll have to be silenced!

I struck my head on the fireplace. He must have thought I was dead and dumped me in the sack.

Why you . . ! Come with me!

Leave her alone . . . *OUCH!*

Out of my way! I won't make the same mistake twice.

You lot keep back if you know what's good for you.

You don't scare us, mister. Let's get him, lads!

23

Let go of me, you ruffians!

Ellie, where are you?

I'll fetch the police.

Oh, Annie, be careful!

AAAH!

Annie. Oh, Annie!

Ellie — your eyes are the brightest blue. Somehow I always imagined they would be.

YOU CAN SEE!

Some weeks later —

Since that toff got arrested, we ain't seen nothing of you, Ellie.

Annie's really an heiress. This is your reward for helping justice take its course.

It's fair shares for all, Ellie. Don't you want yours?

I've already got my reward. I'm leaving here, to live in the country, as Annie's companion.

Once she was my eyes — now she's my best friend. Goodbye, Watt.

THE END

GIRLS! GIRLS! GIRLS!

Have fun with this super Word Search. From the list below, see if you can find the girls' names in our word square. The names may be read up or down, backwards, forwards or diagonally, and letters may be used more than once.
Happy hunting!

```
A N N B C L A R E B L E H C A R C J I A
N T A F B E N I N A J G O I E E B O M R
N R G U Q B E T H C S N V R T D H A I A
N E M M A A D K Y K A N L X B T G O N Y
T N H I O Z R M H I Y A K Z O X E N A R
T Y M F A A P C E S B P A U L I N E L A
T E L O I S E R M A R Y A S A R T N D L B
E X I D K I G E A I O E T B H A U Y I I Z
X E R B H N P R B L K L Y C Z H E L B J B
L A B R E N D A L T R A C Y C Y H A Q R
I I M A J L J N U C H E L E N G L A A M Z
Z A R A L D C D N E V E R A M I R S I H
A R C F E Y Y O W U E S U S A N O A C T
B B T E R A G R A M B A Y A N D B R H E
J E N N I F E R D K A R E N D A E A E B
P O P F E L H A N N A H A G Y X D H L A
E C S J A N I T A B A E F E C H K A L Z
N N F I I H T I D U J F G L O U I S E I
A P A X E K A R O D I A N A M O I R A L
J M C A I L U J A H T N A M A S B L G E
```

Angela
Anita
Ann
Annette
Barbara
Beth
Beverley
Brenda
Charlotte
Clare
Connie
Dawn

Deborah
Diana
Dora
Eliza
Elizabeth
Ellen
Eloise
Emma
Grace
Hannah
Helen
Jane

Janine
Jean
Jennifer
Jill
Joanne
Josie
Judith
Julia
Karen
Kay
Kim
Lily

Linda
Louise
Lucy
Lynne
Mandy
Margaret
Marilyn
Mary
Mia
Michelle
Moira
Pat

Pauline
Rachel
Rita
Rula
Samantha
Sarah
Susan
Sylvia
Tracy
Vera
Yolande
Zara

25

JUNIOR NANNY

IT was Christmas Eve and Nurse Chris Johnson and her colleague, Anne, had taken some of their nursery youngsters out carol singing.

That was lovely, children. Now it really feels like Christmas.

Only cissies believe in Santa Claus! It's just one of the grown-ups dressed up!

No it's not! Santa Claus comes from Greenland on Christmas Eve on his sleigh! So there!

Bobby Fisher says there isn't really a Santa Claus!

Then Santa won't leave him any presents tonight, will he, Peggy?

Bobby's really spoiling Christmas for everyone, Chris.

It appears he's had a rough upbringing, Anne. He's never really known the magic of Christmas.

Bobby wasn't the only one, it seemed —

Go away! You're too early! Can't stand Christmas, anyway!

Sorry we troubled you, Mr Connor. Come along, children. It's time we were getting back now.

We should have known better than to have called on Mr Connor. He's a proper old Scrooge.

I suppose he's lived alone for so long he's forgotten how to enjoy Christmas.

26

If you think there's a Santa Claus, you're a cissy! Ha! Ha! Cissy!

There *IS* a Santa Claus, so there! You're a horror, Bobby Fisher!

Now stop that at once, Bobby!

Later —

Your Santa Claus costume has arrived, Nurse, complete with whiskers.

I was really looking forward to being Santa, but now young Bobby Fisher has spoiled everything.

Never mind Bobby, Anne. The other children will be thrilled. Try on the costume.

The costume's too big. I'm not going to fool *ANY* of the children in this — let alone Bobby!

All you need is a little padding, Anne.

How's that? Ho! Ho! Ho! Merry Christmas, everyone!

Fine Anne, but try to deepen the sound of your voice a bit more.

As the children prepared for bed —

I tell you Santa Claus will be one of the grown-ups dressed up! When he comes in we'll ambush him and pull off his whiskers!

Peggy! You should be in bed and fast asleep by now!

It's Bobby Fisher, Nurse Anne! Him and some of the other boys are going to wait up and ambush Santa Claus! They're going to try to pull off his whiskers!

Is that so?

Thanks for letting us know, Peggy. We'll pass on your message to Santa. I'm sure he'll know how to deal with Bobby.

The little horror! Whoever heard of a child wanting to ambush Santa Claus? He could spoil everything for the other children!

We'll wait until the early hours before we do the rounds. With luck, Bobby will have got tired of waiting and fallen asleep.

Much later—

I thought you'd have dished out the presents and been in your beds by now!

A slight technical hitch, Matron. We're on our way.

I'll go up first and make sure Bobby and his pals are asleep, Anne.

All right. I'll give you five minutes. Oops! I keep losing my padding!

All sound asleep. I had a feeling Bobby would get tired of waiting.

But, as Chris entered the girls' dorm —

What on earth?

There was just one gift left for Bobby —

And what about our unbeliever? Shall I take this present back to Toyland?

You mean you really ARE Santa Claus?

Yes, I really AM Santa Claus! Happy Christmas!

Happy Christmas, Santa!

Anne, you deserve an Oscar for that performance! You were brilliant! Bobby is totally convinced there's a Santa Claus now!

What are you talking about, Chris? I lost my padding. I've had to go back to our room for more string!

You . . . you mean you weren't just up in the dorm letting Bobby swing on your whiskers?

Well, of course I wasn't, Chris! What's going on?

My goodness, look there! I could have sworn that was Santa's sleigh and reindeer!

Matron, what's going on? Do you know something we don't?

I just know that it's Christmas. A time for magic, wouldn't you say? Goodnight!

And, in Mr Connor's cottage —

You should have seen their faces, Tiger, when they tried to pull my beard off! Ha! Ha! This is the happiest Christmas I've had in years!

The End

John was a good laugh—

GERONIMO!

Richard was quieter — he took me for long strolls on the beach—

Simon, on the other hand, liked discos—

Still a week to go. Susie and I will tell you about the other boys when we get home

A week later—

Hi, Jackie. I'm back. Listen — I lied to you in my letter, about all those boys. I did it to get back at you after that row we had.

Oh, Jackie. I'm so sorry. There weren't any boys — honestly.

I know, Julie. Susie told me. That was a stupid row we had. Let's start again, but don't write me any more letters, okay?

The End

34

Mummy's Girl

Continued from Page 13

Why did Trudy run off like that, Janet?

Well . . . er . . .

Janet had no alternative but to tell Mrs Larkin all about Trudy's problem —

I see. Oh, dear me.

Next day—

Let's go to the music room this lunch break, Trudy. You can practise your guitar and I'll just listen.

Okay, if you like.

I hope Mrs Larkin pulls this off alright.

Who's that playing?

It's okay, Trudy. Don't YOU stop.

40

Goldie

I'm just a little mongrel pup
And Goldie is my name,
I have no gracious pedigree
And can't aspire to fame.

But what I have, I gladly give
My love and trust to you
A sympathetic, listening type,
A loyal pal so true.

And as around the fire we sit,
And by your feet I'm curled,
Whate'er I am to you, my friend,
You are to me, my world!

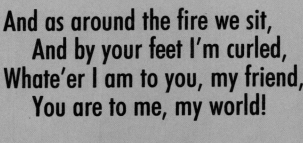

Neighbours

CLEA CORNELL and her mother, an architect, had been looking for an unusual house in the country for some time. In Kirk Rainwood, they saw just what they wanted.

Mother! Just look at that old church! Isn't it beautiful?

It's obviously not been used for years. I could apply to the Church Commissioners. It might be for sale.

Oh, I hope so! It would make a fabulous home!

It's a mess, but the fabric is sound. It shouldn't cost too much to convert, Clea.

What a terrific place to live! And we wouldn't have to worry about the neighbours.

Clea and her mother booked into the village inn—

Let's hope the Commissioners agree to sell, Mother.

We'll soon find out, when they answer this letter.

A week later, they were invited to the Church Commission offices—

The Commissioners have no objection to selling the church building. It has already been deconsecrated.

Then we can buy it?

They're just country people prejudiced against town people. I'll sort them out! See you at the church in an hour.

'Bye, Mother.

The first objector is John Derath, 16 High Street. That must be along here, somewhere.

At the next address—

John Bradbrook, The Dairy, Longthorpe Road. This is Longthorpe Road, but there's no dairy here!

Nobody's lived here for years! It'll be a phoney name, too, I shouldn't wonder!

Next—

Rosamond Hargrave, 27 Well Lane. This leads to the new houses. It might be a real address this time.

It was—

Number 27 is a Wimpy Bar! The old cottage must have been demolished years ago!

Aunt Clarissa and Nellie seem to like each other. All we need do is arrange for Nellie to go shopping with Aunt Clarissa and . . .

Later, Nellie was sent for —

It's just not done to ask outright for a gift, Nellie, and Aunt Clarissa never seems to take our hints, so we need YOU to help us.

Me? But — HOW?

Simple. You'll be sent to help her with her shopping. All you need do is draw her attention to the right things .

Alice and I have made up a list of things we'd like. The rest is up to YOU, Nellie.

Get the idea? It's up to you to draw Aunt Clarissa's attention FORCIBLY to what we think she ought to spend her money on.

But . . .

If you value your job here, you'll do as you are told. One word from us to Mother and you'll be looking for another position — WITHOUT references!

Oh, lawks! What an awful job to lumber me with! Lady Farben isn't daft! She'll tumble what I'm trying to do at once. I'll feel so embarrassed .

The following day —

This just won't work and I'll be out of a job. What CAN I do?

Cheer up, Nellie dear! This is the season of happiness and goodwill.

That's right! And when you see how some other poor people suffer, my silly problems are NOTHING!

Poor people like this woman and her children will be having a very thin Christmas indeed. At least I'll be warm and well fed.

I was saving up to buy myself a little treat for Christmas, but this poor woman needs it more than I do.

Bless you, dear!

Come along, Nellie! I'm waiting!

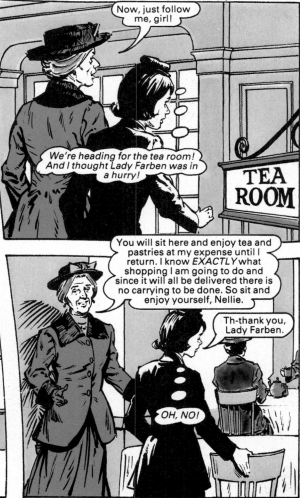

Now, just follow me, girl!

We're heading for the tea room! And I thought Lady Farben was in a hurry!

TEA ROOM

You will sit here and enjoy tea and pastries at my expense until I return. I know EXACTLY what shopping I am going to do and since it will all be delivered there is no carrying to be done. So sit and enjoy yourself, Nellie.

Th-thank you, Lady Farben.

OH, NO!

footer text: 52

When they all arrived at the address —

But . . . there must be some mistake! This can't be for me!

No mistake, my dear! This is a Christmas present from my two nieces Flora and Alice.

WHAT?

I overheard your instructions to dear Nellie when you told her to "draw Aunt Clarissa's attention FORCIBLY to the right things!" Well she DID! I saw her give some money to this poor woman and her needy children.

You will NOT blame Nellie since she did exactly what you told her to do. I think this Christmas present to you both is a good lesson to us all. We should know the true spirit of Christmas — the joy of GIVING.

I don't know HOW to thank you. It'll be the first real Christmas we've known since my husband died. Would . . . would you accept my invitation to share our Christmas dinner tonight . . . you and your friend here?

What do you say, Cook? We'll be finished serving the Selby Smythes by then.

And so —

Miss Flora and Miss Alice DAREN'T take it out on you, Nellie. Aunt Clarissa would come down on them like a ton of bricks!

Actually, I think they were both touched by it. It did 'em good to see how the other half lives.

A happy Christmas to all of us . . . 'specially YOU, Nellie!

The End

53

SHE'S picking on ME! She gave me a slogan for the competition, and now she doesn't want me to use it.

Huh? You gave him a slogan, Bobby? Which one?

Boys — let me explain.

The boys were not amused—

You were SINGING it? OUR slogan?

I — I'm sorry, boys . . . I just didn't think!

Simmons' mother will be able to post his entry when she gets back to London this evening. So it'll arrive before ours.

Later—

Of course! I'll offer Sneaky a choice of the ones the boys didn't want. At least it's a way out of getting thumped by them . . . Ah, here they are!

They blame everything on me! It was that horrible Sneaky Simmons who pinched their slogan. And why can't they use another? They made up about a dozen.

Bobby rushed into town—

You must be Roberta. I've heard all about you.

Er . . . hello, Mrs Simmons. Look, Sneaky — I mean, Simmons — give me back that slogan and you can have your pick of these. They're all good.

Well . . . . I don't know . . .

Hey, I like this one. "Breeze's . . . The Famous Cheese Eaten By Famous People."

That's the one I like. It has real STYLE.

Later, back at Westbury—

. . . so I got Simmons to agree not to use your slogan.

Thanks, Bobby, you're a pal!

I think I was right not to tell them I'd got their slogan back by giving Sneaky ANOTHER one of theirs. They're bound to be a bit sensitive about that for a while.

Boys, tell me — why did you get so upset when you had so many other slogans to choose from?

It's hard to explain, Bobby. But two fellows who intend to make a future in Advertising have got a nose for a prize-winning slogan, right, Don?

Mike's right, Bobby.

The following Saturday, the winning slogan was published—

Here it is. The winning slogan is . . .

Don, listen to this. The winning slogan is "Breeze's The Famous Cheese Eaten By Famous People."

Bobby gave away OUR slogan!

BOBBY! Come back here!

Two hours later—

I wonder if they've calmed down yet. I've thought of another slogan — "Everything comes to she who waits"!

THE END

In Dee

"**C**OME on, Helen!" Sonia cried, dancing about on the hot sand. She could hardly wait to reach the part of the beach near the lifeguards' hut to see if he was here today.

"Where are we going to park ourselves?" asked Helen, catching her up.

Sonia wrinkled her snub nose, thinking hard. It was terribly important to her to get to know that nice new lifeguard with the red hair . . . *really* get to know him, that is. So where they sat on the beach needed a lot of thought.

He wasn't like some of the others who just sat around outside the hut. He patrolled the area, and sometimes sat further down the beach to keep an eye on the people in the water.

"Why don't we sit up near the sand dunes as it's so windy?" Helen suggested.

"All right," Sonia agreed, thinking it was as good a place as any. And later they could always have a game with the beach ball. There was nothing like a ball game to position yourself well so you'd be noticed. She was glad they'd persuaded Helen's little brother, Terry, to lend it to them.

"Mind you look after it," he had said sternly.

"Of course we will!" they'd chorused indignantly.

The flags, blowing straight out towards the sea, were spaced wide apart today so there was a big area for the lifeguards to patrol.

Sonia threw her bag and towel down on the sand, and removed her jeans and shirt. She was glad Mum had let her have a new bikini. Then she caught her breath as she saw him among the other lifeguards, the sunshine glinting on his bright red hair.

Yesterday he'd smiled at her rather hesitantly as if he would have liked to speak, but just then someone had shouted to him to move the flags further up the beach and after that there hadn't been another chance to get near him.

But today was going to be different. Somehow they were going to get together if she had to half drown herself to do it!

Sonia smiled happily, thinking about him. Helen was reaching for Terry's precious beach ball and starting to blow it up, cheeks puffed out. Any minute now she'd be suggesting a game with it.

"How about a game with the ball?" said Helen, right on cue. "What are you grinning at?"

"Nothing. Not much, that is."

And now, suddenly, Sonia didn't feel a bit like smiling. She had just noticed that blonde girl with the suntan down there by the lifeguards' hut. The girl was smiling up at him, and Sonia's heart seemed to skip a beat as she watched them walk down the beach together.

"That's Janice Harper," said Helen, nodding towards the girl. "She comes to Guides. And that must be Nick Henson, the new lifeguard she was telling us about. She thinks he's fantastic."

Hardly aware of what she was doing, Sonia followed Helen down to the harder flatter sand, and they started to throw the ball about. But Sonia missed it again and again.

"What's up with *you*?" asked Helen at last. "Oh, come on! This is no good. Let's go for a swim."

Playing ball or swimming, what did it matter? Helen ran up to place the ball by their pile of clothes, then joined Sonia in the sea. The waves were huge today, and the girls leapt up and down laughing as the sea broke over them. Sonia looked back towards the beach. Nick was alone now. She liked the way his red hair kept flopping over his face so that he had to shake it back.

As another wave broke over her, Sonia came to a quick decision. She'd go up and speak to him this very minute . . . actually say something to him like "Hi!" Well, she hadn't anything to lose . . .

HE was watching someone on a lilo as she approached, and she breathed a sigh of relief as the man on it changed his mind and came back to shore.

"Thank goodness," she said. "I'd hate anything to happen."

"And it could, easily, in a wind like this," he said, turning to smile at her. His brown eyes looked so warm and friendly that she felt she'd known him for ages. "You've no idea how stupid some people are."

She nodded in agreement, but at the same time feeling a little stupid herself because he was so nice to be with.

"Have you been at this long?" she asked.

"Only a week or two. I'm just helping out at the moment."

Water

As he was speaking he was watching the people in the water, and she had the feeling that with him around no one would get into any trouble.

"Have you rescued many people yet?"

"No such luck." He shook his red head and grinned suddenly. "I don't exactly want anyone to get into difficulties, but I'd like a go at rescuing in real life."

He smiled, looking into space in a dreamy kind of way. Perhaps he was thinking about rescuing someone like her . . .

Suddenly he was looking further along the beach.

"I must go along and see what those children are doing on the other side of the flag," he said, giving her that warm smile again before turning and walking away. Sonia watched him go all the way along the beach. Perhaps Janice Harper was along there, too . . .

Then she saw the beach ball rolling down the beach towards her in a sudden gust of wind. She picked it up and threw it as hard as she could to Helen, then ran back into the sea in time to catch it again.

Backwards and forwards the ball flew. Sonia leapt to catch an even higher throw, but missed it and fell back into the breaking wave.

"*Sonia!*" Helen cried in anguish.

There was Terry's precious ball being carried further and further away from Sonia. Quickly she swam after it, but she knew she'd never reach it even before she felt herself getting breathless. She had come further out than she intended and a strong current was pulling her away from the shore.

Really frightened now, Sonia thrashed madly about. Then a hand grabbed her, and she was pulled back towards the beach.

The relief at being in shallow water again made her tremble.

"Are you all right?" Nick asked anxiously.

Sonia nodded dumbly, afraid to look at him in case all she saw in his eyes was the contempt he'd be feeling for her. Janice Harper would never have been such a fool.

They walked out of the water side by side.

"I should have had more sense," she said simply. But how could she act sensibly with Nick around?

And then there was a crowd round them, and there wasn't the chance to say any more.

"What must he think of me?" Sonia thought miserably.

Helen, white-faced, seemed to know without her saying anything that she wanted to go home at once. They didn't talk as they changed back into shirts and jeans, and it wasn't until they had left the hot sand dunes behind them that Sonia spoke.

"I'm sorry about Terry's ball, Helen,"

she said. "We'll get him another one. I'll come round tonight with some money."

She'd really messed things up now, she thought sadly as she walked the rest of the way home alone. Nick wouldn't want to know her now.

If only she had had the sense to let the ball go! It had all happened so quickly, and she hadn't even had the chance to thank him properly.

* *. * *

Even though she knew it wasn't any use thinking of him any more, Sonia found herself wandering down to the beach again on her way to Helen's house that evening. Somehow she felt closer to him here even though there were only acres of empty sand.

The tide was well out, and the wind had dropped . . . the wind that had taken the ball so swiftly out. For ages she stood staring out to sea, wishing with all her heart she hadn't been so stupid.

Then she turned and stood still in amazement. For there, across the hard sand, was her name marked out in large letters . . . SONIA . . . SONIA . . . SONIA.

Then she saw him, stick in hand, looking shamefacedly down at the letters at his feet.

"I didn't expect to see you," he said quietly. "Not after the way you dashed off earlier before I could tell you not to worry. You're not the first to act without thinking . . ."

Sonia felt her face flood with colour.

"I was too ashamed . . ." she began.

And, incredibly, he was smiling at her, his brown eyes warm and friendly.

"The letters will have washed away by morning," he said.

"Not washed away," said Sonia, smiling back. "Just covered by the sea. Invisible writing under the waves."

"And only us two knowing about it," he said.

And then they were walking along the beach together, right to the other end where the cliffs towered above the rock pools, and Nick was explaining all about being a lifeguard as if he really wanted her to understand.

THE END

59

So much for our new neighbours! I shan't be bothering with *THEM* again!

Oh, well, no new friends from next door, that's for sure.

Next morning—

What an awful noise! They ought to keep their dog quiet first thing in the morning!

That dog next door must have wakened the whole street!

Well *I'M* not going round to complain. I want nothing to do with them!

I'll go, Mum.

So—

Hello. I'm Andrew Carter. Sorry about Rex. He's not used to our new home yet.

Well just try and keep him a bit quieter, will you? He woke us all up at the crack of dawn!

I'll try. Sorry again. 'Bye.

Andrew seems very nice. Pity Mum won't have anything to do with his family.

62

I don't know what to say, Pat!

Look, you'll really *HAVE* to do something about Rex!

Just then—

Andrew, what are you — Oh, hello. You must be from next door. I've been meaning to call round.

Er . . . that might not be a good idea, Mrs Carter.

Pat explained about her mother's first visit—

Oh, my goodness! That was your mother who called? I thought it was that doorstep salesman who'd been pestering me all day!

Perhaps you'd better go round and make peace, Mum!

I'll take your mother some of my home-made cake, Pat.

If you want to show Rex around, Andrew, I'd be happy to show you the town.

Great! Hang on while I get his lead.

Pat and Andrew spent a pleasant morning—

And that's the old mill. All the kids think it's haunted.

I think I'm going to like living around here, Pat.

NO TRES

Cinderella Jones

CINDY JONES worked hard at the Happyholme Guest House, owned by her stepmother.

Haven't you finished the cleaning yet, Cindy? You're getting bone idle, girl!

You ARE in a bad temper, Stepmother. Did that snobby Mrs Smye upset you again at the Women's Guild meeting?

I'll teach that woman to talk about me behind my back! Isobelle! Sarah! Claude! Cindy! Into the music room — NOW!

I wonder what's up?

I thought I told you to deliver those Christmas cards, Cindy!

I haven't had time yet. If you weren't too mean to put stamps on them, they would have been delivered ages ago!

You want us, Mother?

Snobby Mrs Smye has been saying that I'm not pulling my weight collecting for charity! Well, we're going to show her. Tonight we are going carol singing!

Carol singing?

What a good idea, The Happyholme Choir!

I'll play my violin!

And I'll play my trumpet!

We'll have a rehearsal! "Good King Wenceslas" after three.

This I've got to hear — UNFORTUNATELY!

Mr Daniels has no family. He's all alone. I expect at Christmas, with everyone enjoying themselves, he feels even more lonely. I've a spare Christmas card here . . . I'll pop it through his door.

What's this?

Tears welled in Mr Daniels' eyes —

We've got a Christmas card, puss. "Happy Christmas from all at Happyholme."

A little later —

ONCE IN ROYAL DAVID'S CITY, STOOD A LOWLY CATTLE SHED . . .

THE FIRST NOEL, THE ANGELS DID SAY . . .

Push off! We were here first, Mrs Smye!

Oh no, you weren't! In any case we're a REAL choir! We've got accompaniment!

Louder, folks! LOUDER!

Accompaniment, eh! Sarah, fetch your violin! Claude, fetch your trumpet!

The two choirs confronted each other —

SING UP!

AWAY IN A MANGER, NO CRIB FOR A BED . . .

LOUDER!

GOOD KING WENCESLAS LOOKED OUT, ON THE FEAST OF STEVEN . . .

CLEAR OFF!

LEAVE US IN PEACE!

EEEK!

YEEOOW!

I guess we had that coming, folks!

Midnight came —

I'll beat that conceited Mrs Smye's total even if I have to fill the tin myself!

That's cheating, Stepmother!

Back at Happyholme, the takings were counted—

Thirteen pounds fifty-three pence, Mrs Jones! And you only collected nine pounds seventy-five! That makes ME the winner!

BAH! I demand a recount!

Stepmother, we have a visitor.

I'm sorry I was rude to you when you sang carols at my home, Mrs Jones. I've been alone so long I've forgotten what it's like to have friends. Please accept this for your charity. And thank you for your Christmas card.

FIVE POUNDS! That makes ME the winner!

Thank you, Mr Daniels. You must come and join us for Christmas dinner tomorrow.

HAPPY CHRISTMAS, EVERYONE!

THE END

Make this
CAT TISSUE BOX

This novel tissue box cover makes a charming gift.

MATERIALS REQUIRED: —

1 A tall box of coloured tissues (Most chemists stock these squarish boxes)

2 A 17″ (435 mm.) square of fur fabric

3 Small pieces of felt for eyes

4 Black felt or cardboard for "pupils"

5 Some glue, suitable for material

6 Black and white thread

TO MAKE: —
FACE — Trace outline of cat's face onto thin card. Cut out. Lay on back of fur fabric and draw round. Ensure that the shape is placed on fabric so that a strip (7″ long x 5½″ deep) can be cut from it later. Allowing a margin of ⅝″ (14 mm.) wider than guideline, cut out fabric. Stick fur onto face-shaped card.

FEATURES
Trace eyes onto card, lay eyes on the felt and cut out. Cut small, round black pupils from felt or cardboard. Sew a small highlight dot in each pupil with white thread before gluing pupils in position, and gluing eyes to face.
Mark nose and mouth, then embroider features with black thread or wool.

TO COVER BOX
Cut a strip of fur fabric 17″ long x 5½″ deep (435 mm. x 140 mm.). Join the two ends together. Cut a square of fur fabric slightly larger than the top of the tissue box. Stick this to the joined piece of fabric to form a box shape. Stick or glue the cat's face to it.

Remove opening tab of tissue box. Place tissue box cover over the box.
Make a slit in the fur at the top. Pull a tissue from the box, through the slit. Now your cat tissue box is ready for use!

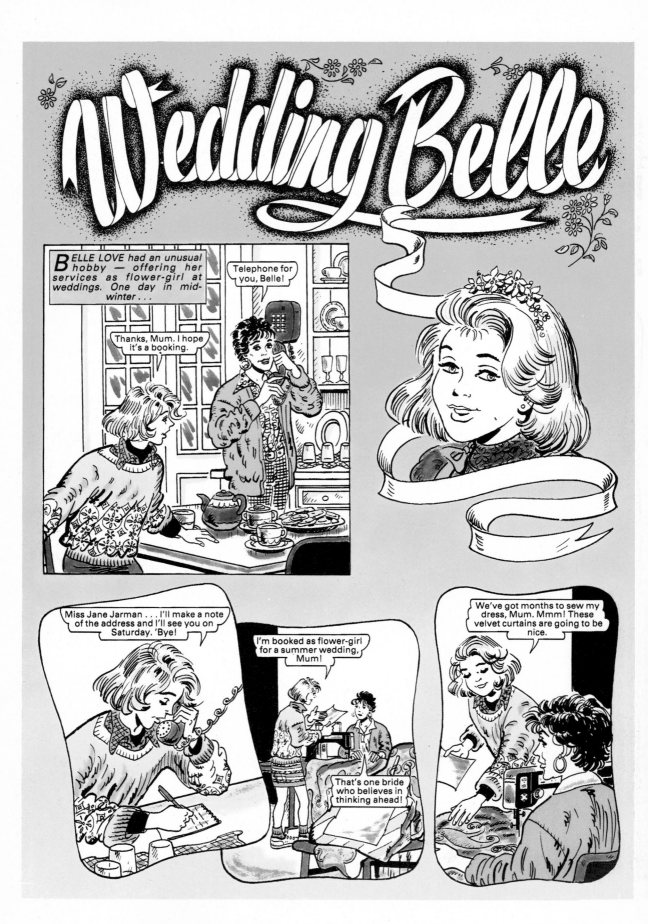

Professor Sinden tested the robots' circuits —

I am your fairy godmother! You shall have a coach and six white horses.

Try on the glass slipper.

Dad, please!

Sorry. I won't be much longer.

Wanda will play the fairy godmother. Tula will play Prince Charming.

A wise choice.

Cindy will play Buttons, and Susie will play the Baroness.

But Buttons is just a common servant!

Twins Fiona and Fenella were upset by the casting —

The UGLY sisters? It's not fair, Sally!

And you, Selena, will play Cinderella.

Great!

You were bound to choose her. She's your twin, Sally!

That afternoon, Sally and her sisters went to the village hall for a dress rehearsal —

Clean out the grate, Cinders! Put your back into it, girl!

It's amazing the way your sisters have learned their parts so quickly, Sally.

This heater is pretty old, Vicar, but I've managed to fix it for you.

Thank you. The central heating's not too good. I didn't want our audience to be cold tonight.

That evening —

Looks like we've got a full house, Dad. You're sure nothing can go wrong?

Of course not, Sally. Your sisters have been fully programmed to play their parts. Stop worrying.

GROW YOUR OWN HERBS

Why not grow some herbs to use in the kitchen? They add lovely flavours to salads, sauces, soups and stews. For those without a garden, herbs can be grown in window boxes, and some do well inside, on a window sill.

To start your herb garden, you will need:
packets of seeds, seed and cutting compost, grit sand, plastic trays (or foil take-away containers), seed pots (or yoghurt pots with holes bored in the bottom). Get an adult to help you do this.

Place a small quantity of grit sand in the bottom of the small pots and then fill them up with the compost. Scatter the seeds on top and stand the pots in a tray of water until the compost becomes damp.

Place the tray in a warm dark place. (An airing cupboard is ideal). Some seeds will start to sprout in a matter of days. Others will take up to three weeks. Once the herbs have sprouted, place the pots on a window sill that gets lots of sun and light. Keep the compost moist, but not wet. When the seedlings are big enough to handle, they can easily be removed and replanted in the garden or window box to give each one room to develop.

Amongst the easier herbs to grow are parsley, mint, sage, chives and fennel. Once your plants are established and healthy, they can be used for cooking. So out with the recipe books!

COMPOST

GRIT SAND

FENNEL

CHIVES

PARSLEY

SAGE

THYME

TARRAGON

MINT

Danny's out and Karen's out, after they both told me they were staying in. It can't be a coincidence. They must be together.

But surely they wouldn't do that? Not my best friend and my boyfriend. I'm being ridiculous, and jumping to all the wrong conclusions!

I'll go over to Janice's house and copy the homework exercise numbers from her.

But, as Tricia neared the town centre—

It's a nuisance she's not on the phone. Still, it won't take me long to walk.

There's Danny with Karen! I WAS right after all. They ARE out together!

Tricia ran homewards in tears—

I thought Danny cared about me. And Karen's been my best friend for years! How COULD they?

It just shows, you can't trust anyone. All the time Karen was telling me she thought Danny and I were really suited, she was dating him behind my back!

I'm so upset — and it's Christmas, too! What a rotten lonely Christmas it's going to be for me with no boyfriend and no best friend any more!

The next morning—

I must get to school early so I can do that Maths homework before lessons start.

In the classroom—

Phew! That's the last question finished, thank goodness. Oh! Someone's coming in.

In the playground—

There's Karen. Luckily she hasn't seen me. I don't ever want to speak to her again.

86

The Lonely Limpet

Down in a rock pool,
   Underneath a stone,
There sat a little limpet
   Who lived all alone.

Suddenly a storm came,
   The water flowed so high,
Big waves came a-rushing,
   And almost touched
          the sky!

Then the sea went back again,
   The water ran away,
No more wicked whistling wind,
   And no more salty spray.

In the little rock pool,
    The sand began to clear,
And then our lonely
            limpet friend
    Gave out a hearty cheer.

A host of little fishy friends,
    Were peering through the gloom,
"Welcome," cried the limpet,
    "Welcome to my room."

"I've been here so very long,
    The limpet said aloud,
"But now I've got a happy heart,
    Because I'm with a crowd."

SHELTER from the STORM

FROM the moment she'd arrived in Branmawr, on holiday with her family, Penny Fox had been fascinated by the deserted house on the beach.

Doesn't it look mysterious and quiet?

It looks like rain. We'd better pack up.

Spooky, more like, Penny! A boy in the village was telling me no one ever goes there.

I think I'll walk along the beach, Mum. See you back at the hotel. I'll shelter if the rain gets too heavy.

I really wanted a closer look at the house, but now there's a real squall blowing up.

As Penny approached the house—

Oh! Someone's crying!

There's a boy in the old house! He looks so miserable!

What was it like at the orphanage, Jason?

It's strange, Penny! When — when I try to think about it, my mind gets hazy. It's as if . . . as if it all happened long ago. Yet it was only last winter I was there!

At that moment—

There you are, Sarge, just as I said! There's smoke coming from the chimney, and we know no one's living there.

Must be some kids mucking about. We'll have a word with them. They could burn the place down.

Inside the house—

Listen! Someone's coming. You stay here and I'll see who it is.

Yes, Penny. I'll stay here, where it's warm.

Now, what's going on here, miss? I'm Sergeant Harris from the local police station.

Oh, Sergeant, I'm so glad you're here! There's a poor boy inside called Jason Stark. His boat, the "Mary-Ann Martin", went down, and he's been half drowned.

We lit a fire because he was so cold. He's in here.

Wait a minute, love. *WHAT* did you say the name of the boat was?

93

The — the "Mary-Ann Martin".

But the "Mary-Ann Martin" went down many years ago, in my FATHER'S time.

That's right, Sarge. My grandad used to talk about it. Only one of the crew was lost. The lifeboat picked up the rest.

A lad from the orphanage, name of Jason Stark, was the one who drowned.

His body was found in this very house. He survived the shipwreck and sheltered here from the storm but died of exposure before he was found.

That . . . that CAN'T be right! He was here a minute ago! See? The fire's burning!

I . . . I don't understand. Jason WAS here!

Reckon you must have dozed off and dreamt it, love.

No, Sarge . . . LOOK! It . . . it's the wet print of a sea boot. The girl's wearing shoes, and her feet are much smaller!

The mark's drying rapidly. It'll soon be gone. Just a freak coincidence that it looks like a footprint.

I suppose so, Sarge. But, for a moment there, I wondered . . . Never mind, it's time you were getting back to your folks, lass.

At the doorway, Penny turned and looked back—

Goodbye, Jason. I'm glad we met. The fire will burn for a while yet and keep you warm and dry.

THE END

GRANNY'S HOME HELP

YOU REQUIRE

a wooden spoon
2 metal scouring pads
2 all purpose cloths or dish cloths
a duster
safety pins
the bottom of a cardboard egg box
the foot of an old nylon flesh-coloured stocking
a piece of thin card
a fragment of lace (optional)

TO MAKE

Draw a face and neck, with joining strip. (For approx. sizes see Fig.1). Mark features distinctly. Colour cheeks and mouth. Wind side strips of neck round the spoon handle, making sure that the face covers the bowl of the spoon. Hold in position with fine string or thread.

FOR YOU TO MAKE

Granny's Home Help makes a good, practical gift and also sells well at charity fêtes and fairs.

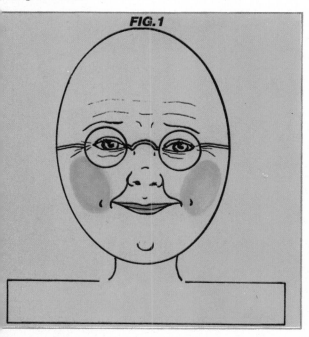

FIG.1

Stretch nylon foot over head. Pad the back with some cotton wool or toilet paper and tack fullness at back of head to neaten. This won't show as it will be covered with a "shawl". Make a hole in either end of the egg box, lengthwise, and push the spoon handle through the egg box.

Now Granny's Home Help has a body! (See Fig.2).

Wind an all purpose cloth round lower part for a skirt. Fasten at back with a safety pin. Wind duster around top half for a shawl. Fix with a safety pin. Stitch metal scouring pads with *LONG* stitches to head (Fig.1). Remember it all has to be undone to use.

Cover head with an all purpose cloth headcovering and fix at the back. Fasten lace at neck.

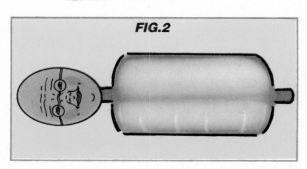

FIG.2

Now Granny's Home Help is ready to go to work! Some people might think she's too pretty to undo!

Judy & Co.

96

SECRET ADMIRER

LEONIE MARTIN had recently moved house and was finding it hard to make friends at her new school. One evening—

Come on, Leonie. Come into the shop with me.

You know you don't want to buy anything, Christi. We've been in three times tonight already!

Christi's such a flirt, but I can't help wishing I was just a little like her. She's got so much confidence and she always seems to be in fashion.

Later —

I bet he thought you were a right wally, playing classical music.

Well, we don't ALL like pop music!

Isn't that a different pair of earrings from the ones you had on half an hour ago, Christi?

Fancy you noticing that, Gary.

You're the new girl at Frampton High, aren't you? My sister, Helen, goes there. Don't you play classical music on the piano?

Er . . . yes, that's right.

It's only a matter of time before Gary asks me out. I'm sure he would have done tonight, if you hadn't been there.

Cheek! You pestered me all evening to go in and out of that shop with you! Well, don't ask me to do it again!

Next morning —

Hi, Leonie. Get all your homework done last night?

She's very chatty, after that little row we had. Still, I suppose I ought to let bygones be bygones.

97

At lunchtime —

You see that girl over there? She's Gary's sister. I want you to go and give her a message.

Why don't you go and give it to her yourself?

Do what I say or you can find yourself another friend! This has got my telephone number on it so that Gary can ring me.

Oh, all right!

Christi's a real pain. I wish I could find someone else to go round with.

Excuse me, but Christi Beecham asked me to give you this for your brother.

Oh, hi! I'm Helen. Aren't you Leonie Martin, the girl who plays the piano?

Er . . . well, yes.

You're great. I've heard you play. Gary and I both love classical music. He's studying it at college.

Really? I thought Gary worked at the shop.

No, just a couple of evenings a week. He did mention that he'd met you but he didn't say anything about your friend. I'll give him her number, but I doubt if he'll ring her.

When Leonie reported back to Christi—

Oh, don't pay any attention to her. She's just winding you up about Gary mentioning you. You couldn't expect him to look at you when I'M around.

98

Next morning —

Just for a moment there I thought Gary might like ME. But Christi's right, I've no chance with him.

Did Gary phone you last night then?

No, but that's because he doesn't want to seem too pushy. I'm going round to the shop tonight. He'll ask me then.

I think I'll get him to take me to see that new movie on Friday.

I know I shouldn't, but I wish it were me he was taking.

Aw, don't look so sad. You're not his type anyway.

Oh, shut up, Christi. I'm sick of your comments. In fact, a boy I've fancied for ages has asked me out on Friday.

Well, there's only one place open on a Friday night in Frampton — and that's the cinema. We'll see you and your boyfriend there on Friday.

Oh, no! Why did I have to pretend like that? Now I'm going to look really stupid.

On Friday evening —

Leonie! Telephone for you!

That'll be Christi ringing to ask what time I'll be at the cinema. How am I going to get out of this? I'll have to say I'm not feeling well.

The Little Donkey

THE little donkey watched as the newcomer was led into the field. He looked admiringly at him and noted the jet black coat gleaming with health. The new arrival pranced up and down, head high as if to say, "Hey, look how handsome I am!" The little donkey had to agree that he undoubtedly was.

The little donkey just stood there, in his corner, watching. He turned his head away to look at his own rough, dull grey coat. The other horses strolled across to greet the thoroughbred. After all, it was not often that such a fine specimen arrived in their field.

The thoroughbred was very proud of himself and he held his fine head as high as he could. He lifted his tail gracefully. For a while there was such a lot of neighing and snorting, that the little donkey began to feel quite annoyed. The

field was open to anyone but he disliked show-offs. He had no intention of going over to make a fuss over this new horse.

Later, the little donkey felt warm. The unusually strong sun had made him thirsty so he slowly walked to the water trough at the other end of the field. Out of the corner of his eye, he saw the thoroughbred, distracted now from all his prancing and showing off. He, too, trotted over towards the trough.

The water looked cool and inviting. Just as the little donkey was about to drink, the thoroughbred was there. With a swish of his tail, a swing of his slim rump, he pushed the little donkey out of the way.

The donkey stood quietly, trying to hold on to his dignity. He had no intention of stooping to that level. He watched the

thoroughbred drinking very slowly, as if he enjoyed making the donkey wait. The little donkey did wait. Patience had always been his strong point.

At last the thoroughbred had had enough. The donkey watched as he swished and swaggered his way back, eyed curiously, of course, by all the other horses. The donkey slowly drank his fill and then plodded on back to his quiet corner of the field. He lay down to have a doze in the late afternoon sun.

After a while the little donkey heard children's voices. He lazily lifted his head to see what was going on, and looked over by the fence where some children were stroking the thoroughbred's silky mane. He watched the black horse nuzzle up to them. "He loves it", thought the donkey, wondering what it must be like to have people make a fuss of you like that. After all, no one had ever made such a fuss of *him*.

The donkey looked on sadly, as the children fed carrots to the thoroughbred. One or two of the other horses were given carrots too.

The little donkey couldn't be bothered to join in, and stayed in his lonely corner just watching, as the thoroughbred was being given apples to munch. "No one has ever given me an apple," he thought.

Soon the sun disappeared behind a cloud, night fell and the field was quiet. Only the sound of trees blowing in the wind, and the owls hooting, interrupted the donkey's lonely silence as he drifted off to sleep.

NEXT morning, the donkey listened to the sounds of a new day. He watched a fieldmouse as it scuttled along in front of him, in search of food. He listened to the birds as they broke into their morning chorus, thinking how content they all seemed, and wondering why he was not.

The little donkey got up to stretch his short, stubby legs, then wandered over to the trough for his morning drink. He was first up, so, undisturbed, he trotted round and round the field, enjoying the early morning exercise. Then, feeling refreshed, he began his breakfast of fresh, juicy grass.

Just as the donkey was enjoying his morning nibble, he heard movement in the far corner of the field. The thoroughbred was up and about. The donkey could also hear voices from the other end, by the fence. The two children had brought something for the thoroughbred. One held a saddle, the other a bridle.

The donkey watched enviously, as the thoroughbred pranced over. He saw the children put the saddle on the sleek back, and secure it firmly. He watched the bridle go on, as the children patted and stroked the thoroughbred's dark mane. The children spoke to him gently. He even had a name — Star. A name . . . now that was something the donkey had never had. Not one that he knew of, anyway. Lonely and rejected, the donkey saw the children lead the thoroughbred out of the field and then trotted back to his quiet corner.

Much later, after a long and lonely day, he heard the children's voices again. He looked across as they led the thoroughbred back into the field. The donkey tried not to look, but couldn't help it, as the thoroughbred pranced up and down on his newly clipped and polished hooves.

But the donkey couldn't take his eyes off what he saw next. No wonder the thoroughbred was showing off. The little donkey watched as the children removed the bright red rosette from his bridle. They stroked him lovingly. The other horses trotted up too, as if to congratulate the recent arrival on his win. Now that was really something. The little donkey desperately wanted to join in the celebrations. But somehow, he just couldn't. For the first time in his entire life, he found himself wishing he was different. He hung his head low feeling very unhappy and dejected.

That evening, it got colder and he knew winter was well on the way. The little donkey was glad of his warm straw. He could shelter in the makeshift shed in the corner that acted as a stable.

Of course, the new pony had a proper stable, with a door, and lots of fresh hay to munch, and straw to snuggle up in. *He* even had a coat. The donkey had seen the children place the thick, warm blanket lovingly on the thoroughbred's back.

THE snow came. It was an effort to keep warm. Then, one crisp, snowy morning, the children came again to the field. At first the little donkey took no notice of them. But, to his surprise, he saw the children make their way down the field towards him, the little donkey.

Even the thoroughbred looked shocked, as they walked straight past him, towards the little donkey. They placed a halter gently around his thick, strong neck. He felt their soft, warm hands caress him. He allowed himself to be led away. He didn't know where or why. But it had to be something nice. He just sensed it.

The school hall was in chaos. Voices were raised. All was hustle and bustle. The little donkey had never seen so many people. He let them put the little girl on his sturdy back. He allowed them to lead him up and down. "Mary," he heard them call her. Yes, that was a nice name.

People began to pile into the hall. The little donkey wondered how they'd all fit in. But they did. He listened to the footsteps, the scraping of chairs; to the incessant chatter and the excitement. The little donkey wasn't sure why he was here, but he was enjoying it.

Suddenly all was quiet. It was time. The children came for him. The donkey wondered why they were dressed up in funny clothes. Once more they placed the halter on his neck. They lifted Mary up onto his strong back. Again they led him up and down. But this time everyone was singing and looking at *him*.

He heard them singing, "Little donkey, carry Mary, safely on her way." Everyone was singing about *him*, the little donkey.

They all looked on as the boy helped Mary down from the donkey's back. He was led into the little cardboard stable where he stood silently. He sensed that he should keep very quiet, and he was right.

Just like everyone else, the little donkey listened and waited. The hall was hushed. The baby cried. As Mary rocked her new-born in her arms, the donkey felt so proud. He was part of it all.

Now he too had a name — "Mary's donkey".

The End

The Perfect Prefect

As it was nearing Christmas, the girls of 3D at Thornton High School had taken a collection . . .

You've done very well, 3D! Which charity is going to benefit from your generosity?

The local children's home, Miss Mitchell. Nicola and I have been chosen to take the money along there this afternoon.

But, when the girls arrived —

Oh, no! There's been a fire, Di!

Oh, I hope no one has been hurt.

I'll have to ask you to use the other entrance, girls. This way is closed.

Thornton's generosity is much appreciated, girls. This is one piece of good news on an otherwise black day.

How bad was the fire, Matron?

Only one small block was affected, but unfortunately, that's where the children's Christmas presents were stored.

106

Then —

STAGE

What's going on? You lot'll be for it when the Head finds out you're in here! The hall's out of bounds unless you've got special permission.

Which we *HAVE*, actually!

That'll teach Becky to interfere! She's the bossiest prefect in the school!

Nicola told her all about the panto—

A panto! Which one?

Well . . . we haven't actually decided yet.

That's the first thing you ought to sort out. Who's in charge here?

Er . . . no one, really.

You lot are hopeless! You need a director to organise things. I'll do it!

You! But you can't! Er . . . what I mean is, surely you're too busy?

Prefects do have a lot of duties, it's true. But I'll make time to help, as it's for such a good cause.

Oh, no! This is going to be awful!

The next day —

I've decided we'll do Cinderella. It's so spectacular. Now, I want you to take it in turns reading from your scripts, so that I can decide who'll be suitable for which part.

Reading out loud? It's just like an English lesson.

Boring!

At least she would be if she'd remembered her cue. Actually she's backstage, filling her face!

Sorry! I didn't realise.

Concentrate Di! Now we'll have to do the whole scene again.

That was awful. Becky's too tough on us!

I agree. I wish she'd never got involved.

This is all your fault, Di. YOU thought of it.

I know what you mean. I'd give up now, but it's the children at the Home who'd suffer. I thought doing a panto would be fun, but it isn't turning out that way. Having Becky involved is a right drag!

Then came the dress rehearsal —

You sit here beside me to watch, Jacki. You can make sure all the costumes look right.

Oh! Who's that?

Your fairy godmother.

What a great entrance!

Everything has gone really well. It's all beginning to come together.

What did you think?

It was ace! We've all moaned about Becky, because she kept on and on going over things until they were perfect. But it's really paid off now. The show's great!

And a few days later, the audience thought so too —

Bravo!

Well done!

Look at the money we've made for the Children's Home.

Thank you all very much, girls. I don't know what we'd have done without you.

The show was a sell-out!

We have Becky to thank, you know. She made sure the show was perfect, even if it did seem a pain at the time.

Maybe we ought to buy her a thank-you present.

Make This
TRINKET TRAY

Here's a great way to keep your earrings, jewellery and other trinkets neat and tidy. It's simple to make, and looks good, too!

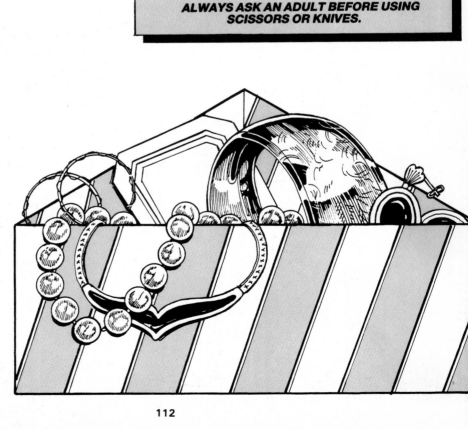

158 mm.

375 mm.

120 mm.

15 mm.

57 mm.

15 mm.

YOU WILL NEED:
Hallmark giftwrap (1 sheet, any design)
Card (380 mm x 160 mm)
Scotch Spray mount adhesive
Double sided Sellotape
Craft knife

1. Cut giftwrap in half and spray back with spray adhesive. Stick smoothly to both sides of card. Draw shape on to giftwrap, taking care to check sizes, and cut out.
2. Score right side along dotted lines with tip of craft knife, taking care not to cut through to wrong side.
3. Bend backwards along the scored lines.
4. Stick side tab inside opposite end with double sided Sellotape, forming a triangle.
5. Stick base tabs under base with double sided tape.
6. Now your trinket tray is complete and ready to use.

ALWAYS ASK AN ADULT BEFORE USING SCISSORS OR KNIVES.

I'm just going to put this over your mouth. It will help you breathe more easily.

Careful with this little lad, Nurse. He has a broken leg.

Later, at St Margaret's —

Well, young man, it's time we had a few particulars! What's your name?

I'm not telling you! Go away!

Meanwhile —

Do you think they're related, Doctor? The boy won't tell us his name!

The woman hasn't been able to tell us anything either. She won't be in any state to do so for a day or two.

But, we'll soon find out who they are. Someone at the flats will be able to tell us!

That evening —

It's no use, Lee. He won't speak to anyone.

I hope so. The young boy seems very unhappy.

Leave it to me. I'm rather good with children.

115

You weren't by yourself, Timmy. Mr Smithers was always there. I know he is your teacher, but he's very fond of you.

YOU weren't there, were you? Or Dad! You're always away.

You won't run away again, Timmy! Promise! Please!

On Christmas Eve —

Well, you're going home today, Mrs Mason. Timmy, too.

All right, Mum! I didn't want to leave home. I just wanted you or Dad to be there with me.

I'm not going home, Nurse! It needs re-decorating after that fire. I'm going to stay with Timmy and his mother for a while.

Mind you, it's done some good! That fire really upset Rene! That and Timmy running away from home! I think she'll spend more time with him now.

Too busy to notice! You let her off lightly, Betsy!

Well, she's had enough trouble lately! Maybe more than we realise.

Haven't I seen you before somewhere, Nurse?

Only once. I was shaking a collecting-box! I think you were too busy to notice.

117

After Lights Out...

This is it, Alex! Langmoor Girls' Academy!

LANGMOOR GIRLS' ACADEMY

THIRTEEN-YEAR-OLD Alex Johnston was about to enroll at Langmoor Girls' Academy where she was to become a boarder . . .

Oh, dear! I've been looking forward to starting at Boarding School for ages, but now the day's actually come, I feel really nervous.

In the headmistress's office—

Hello, Alex. I'm sure you'll be very happy at Langmoor.

Th-thank you, Miss Webster.

I think Alex is anxious about starting at the school in the middle of a term. But her father and I have to go abroad on business rather suddenly, so we've no option.

Of course, Mrs Johnston. I quite understand.

There's really no need for you to worry, Alex. I'm sure you'll find our girls very friendly.

I hope so.

Ah! Here are Carol and Pippa. They'll show you round.

Goodbye darling! Have a lovely time.

By the time Alex's unpacking was finished, it was late —

Quick! We've only two minutes before lights out.

I can't believe it's bedtime already. The day's flown by.

Goodnight, girls. Sleep well.

Goodnight, Miss Buckley.

I ought to sleep well tonight. I'm really tired after all the excitement.

But—

I've been tossing and turning for ages. I just can't drop off. Maybe it's being in a different bed, or all the excitement . . .

Everyone else is asleep. I'll pop along to the washroom and fetch a glass of water. That might help me to nod off.

I think this is the right door. Oh!

x

x

Sorry! Did I startle you? I bet you couldn't sleep. Me neither. I'm Gina Gregory, by the way.

Alex Johnston. I'm new. It's my first day here.

New, eh? What do you think of the place? Langmoor used to be a stately home. Imagine living here then!

It must have been very grand.

Yes, but not very happy. About a hundred years ago, there was a family called Morton living here. They had a daughter about our age. She fell in love with the stable lad, and he loved her too.

"But her father got to hear of it and was furious. There was a fight . . .

. . . and the stable lad was killed."

They reckon the stable lad still haunts the place. Maybe he's looking for revenge.

Ugh! I hope not!

Then—

Oh! What's that noise? It sounds like ghostly footsteps!

It's Miss Buckley doing her last round more likely. We'd better be going. There'll be trouble if we're caught in here.

'Bye!

Goodbye, Gina.

WASHROOM

I wish we were in the same dorm. I don't want to wander round the corridors on my own after Gina's story.

Phew! Made it back to bed. I'm still a bit frightened though.

I'll have to bury my head under the blankets. It's the only way I'll ever get to sleep.

125